South Shore School
4800 S. Henderson St.
Seattle, WA 98118

The United Nations
Global Leadership

Decolonization: Dismantling
Empires and Building Independence

The Five Permanent Members of the Security Council:
Responsibilities and Roles

The History and Structure of the United Nations:
Development and Function

Humanitarian Relief Operations:
Lending a Helping Hand

International Security: Peacekeeping and
Peace-Building Around the World

Pioneering International Law:
Conventions, Treaties, and Standards

UN Action Against Terrorism: Fighting Fear

The UN and Cultural Globalization:
One World, Many People

The UN and the Global Marketplace:
Economic Developments

UNICEF and Other Human Rights Efforts:
Protecting Individuals

The UN and Cultural Globalization

One World, Many People

by Sheila Nelson

Mason Crest Publishers
Philadelphia

Mason Crest Publishers Inc.
370 Reed Road
Broomall, Pennsylvania 19008
(866) MCP-BOOK (toll free)
www.masoncrest.com

Copyright © 2007 by Mason Crest Publishers. All rights reserved. No part of this publication may be reproduced or transmitted in any form or by any means, electronic or mechanical, including photocopying, recording, taping, or any information storage and retrieval system, without permission from the publisher.

13 12 11 10 09 08   10 9 8 7 6 5 4 3 2

Library of Congress Cataloging-in-Publication Data

Nelson, Sheila.
  The UN and cultural globalization : one world, many people / by Sheila Nelson.
     p. cm. — (The United Nations—global leadership)
  Includes bibliographical references and index.
  ISBN 978-1-4222-0072-8   ISBN 978-1-4222-0065-0 (series)
  1. Globalization—Juvenile literature. 2. United Nations—Juvenile literature. I. Title: United Nations and cultural globalization. II. Title. III. Series.
  JZ1318.N45 2007
  341.23—dc22
                        2006001497

Interior design by Benjamin Stewart.
Interiors produced by Harding House Publishing Service, Inc.
www.hardinghousepages.com
Cover design by Peter Culatta.
Printed in the Hashemite Kingdom of Jordan.

Contents

Introduction 6
1. What Is Globalization? 9
2. Globalization and the Environment 19
3. Globalization and Health 29
4. Globalization and Poverty 37
5. Globalization and Religion 47
6. Globalization and the United Nations 57
7. The Future of the United Nations 65
Time Line 74
Glossary 76
Further Reading 78
For More Information 79
Reports and Projects 81
Bibliography 82
Index 85
Picture Credits 87
Biographies 88

Introduction
by Dr. Bruce Russett

The United Nations was founded in 1945 by the victors of World War II. They hoped the new organization could learn from the mistakes of the League of Nations that followed World War I—and prevent another war.

The United Nations has not been able to bring worldwide peace; that would be an unrealistic hope. But it has contributed in important ways to the world's experience of more than sixty years without a new world war. Despite its flaws, the United Nations has contributed to peace.

Like any big organization, the United Nations is composed of many separate units with different jobs. These units make three different kinds of contributions. The most obvious to students in North America and other democracies are those that can have a direct and immediate impact for peace.

Especially prominent is the Security Council, which is the only UN unit that can authorize the use of military force against countries and can require all UN members to cooperate in isolating an aggressor country's economy. In the Security Council, each of the big powers—Britain, China, France, Russia, and the United States—can veto any proposed action. That's because the founders of United Nations recognized that if the Council tried to take any military action against the strong opposition of a big power it would result in war. As a result, the United Nations was often sidelined during the Cold War era. Since the end of the Cold War in 1990, however, the Council has authorized many military actions, some directed against specific aggressors but most intended as more neutral peacekeeping efforts. Most of its peacekeeping efforts have been to end civil wars rather than wars between countries. Not all have succeeded, but many have. The United Nations Secretary-General also has had an important role in mediating some conflicts.

UN units that promote trade and economic development make a different kind of contribution. Some help to establish free markets for greater prosperity, or like the UN Development Programme, provide economic and technical assistance to reduce poverty in poor countries. Some are especially concerned with environmental problems or health issues. For example, the World Health Organization and UNICEF deserve great credit for eliminating the deadly disease of smallpox from the world. Poor countries especially support the United Nations for this reason. Since many wars, within and between countries, stem from economic deprivation, these efforts make an important indirect contribution to peace.

Still other units make a third contribution: they promote human rights. The High Commission for Refugees, for example, has worked to ease the distress of millions of refugees who have fled their countries to escape from war and political persecution. A special unit of the Secretary-General's office has supervised and assisted free elections in more than ninety countries. It tries to establish stable and democratic governments in newly independent countries or in countries where the people have defeated a dictatorial government. Other units promote the rights of women, children, and religious and ethnic minorities. The General Assembly provides a useful setting for debate on these and other issues.

These three kinds of action—to end violence, to reduce poverty, and to promote social and political justice—all make a contribution to peace. True peace requires all three, working together.

The UN does not always succeed: like individuals, it makes mistakes . . . and it often learns from its mistakes. Despite the United Nations' occasional stumbles, over the years it has grown and moved forward. These books will show you how.

Because of modern transportation and communication, the Earth seems like a smaller place today than it did in past centuries.

Chapter 1

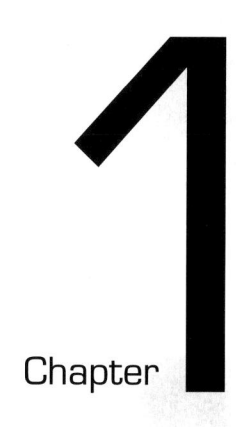

What Is Globalization?

Have you ever heard people say, "It's a small world"? What do they mean by that? After all, the Earth is 24,902 miles (40,076 km.) around the equator—which isn't actually all that small.

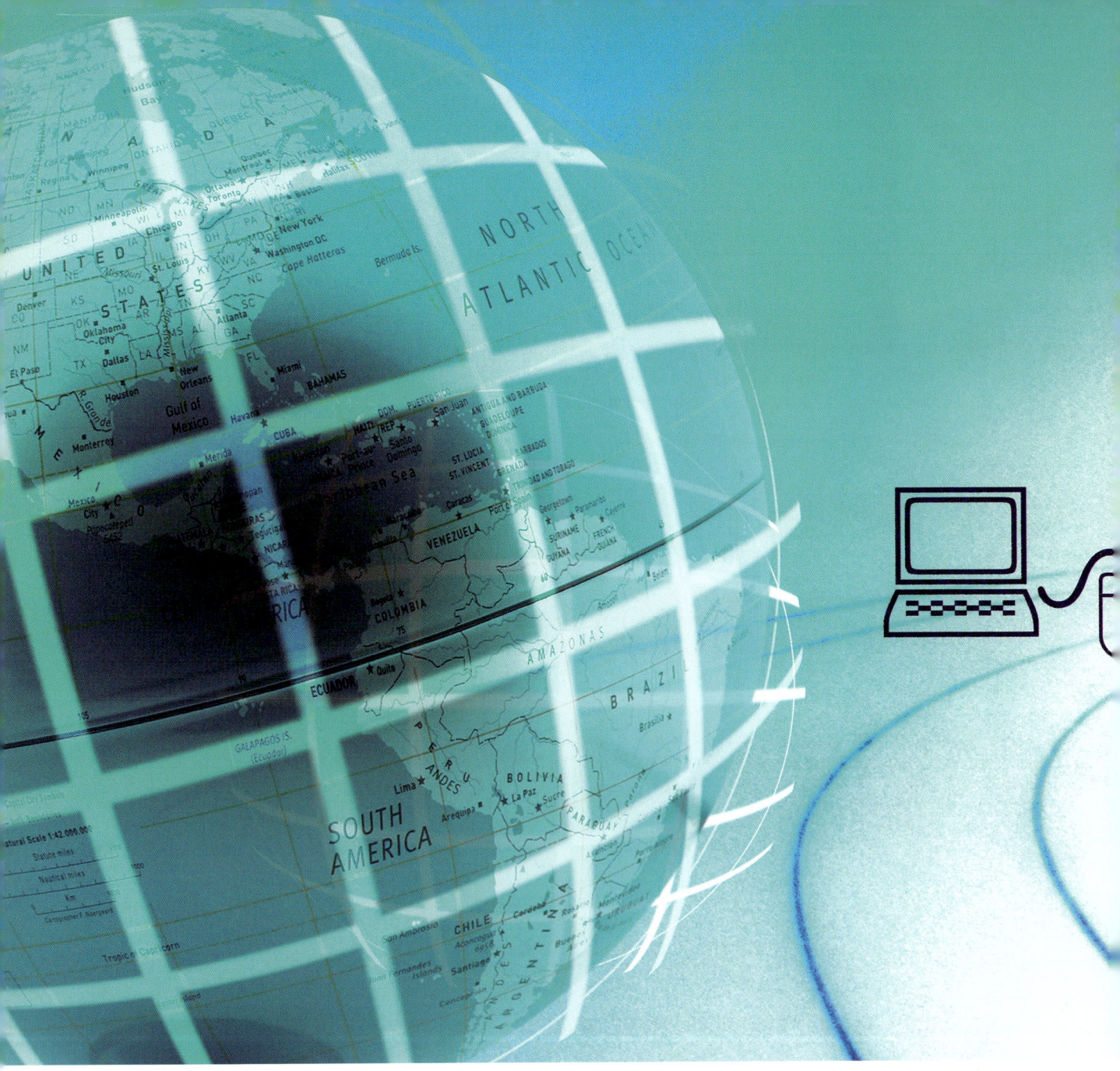

The Internet connects the world.

Chapter One—What Is Globalization?

Hundreds of years ago, people were not sure what lay on the other side of the world, or even if there was another side of the world. The Earth seemed like a vast and mysterious place. In the fifteenth century, explorers mapped out most of the globe, but travel to distant places took months. Communication was slow and uncertain. People in different parts of the world lived very different kinds of lives. They spoke different languages, ate different foods, wore different clothes, and had different traditions.

As technology became more advanced, things such as transportation and communication became quicker and easier. Today, all someone needs to do to talk to people from around the world is pick up a phone. Traveling halfway around the globe now takes hours instead of months, and is relatively safe.

Globalization describes the process of connecting different parts of the world. Sometimes a certain part of the world will be more affected than others by these connections, and sometimes one type of connection will be strongly felt in an area while other types of connections are barely noticeable in that same area. An example would be during a war, when there are many military connnections but not very many economic ones.

Media and the Internet

American movies are shown across the world. Books by international writers are translated into dozens of languages and read by thousands of people. Independent filmmakers in Africa or the Middle East submit their works to international film festivals, offering glimpses into their world and life. The media has allowed people to see into other cultures, encouraging diversity and acceptance of worldwide differences. Some complain, however, that since it is usually American media distributed across the globe the world is not becoming more multicultural but instead is becoming "Americanized."

The Internet has made a huge impact on the spread of information and ideas. Now, people with Internet access can almost instantly reach information on nearly every imaginable subject. A student in the United States can look up Web pages describing a crisis in Africa, while an Asian businessperson might read the financial reports of a competitor half a world away. Never has so much information been so easily available to so many people.

The UN and Cultural Globalization: One World, Many People

Cultural Globalization

The idea of globalization can be very complicated and involves many different aspects. The term "cultural globalization" refers to the effects of many different types of globalization taken together. Different aspects of globalization, which can be examined separately, interact to create a total picture of cultural globalization.

Some of the different areas affecting cultural globalization include trade and the flow of goods across international borders, technological advances leading to faster and better communication and travel between different parts of the world, and the spread of ideas across the globe. These things all work together. For example, travel and communication have become so much easier in the last century that knowledge about different parts of the world has drastically increased. This has led to an increased understanding about different cultures as well as a desire to improve trade and diplomatic ties between nations.

Multiculturalism and cultural ***diversity*** also result from cultural globalization. Today in large cities you can find restaurants serving food from almost everywhere in the world. Grocery stores stock international foods as well. Music from dozens of different countries is available. Many cities have sections where most residents are from a certain part of the world—such as Chinatown or Little Italy. The people who live in these areas hold the traditional festivals of their native countries, eat traditional foods, and sometimes wear traditional clothing.

Economic Globalization

One specific type of globalization is economic globalization, involving money and finances. Economic globalization can be seen, for example, in trade agreements such as NAFTA—the free trade agreement between the United States, Canada, and Mexico. This allows for goods and money to flow across borders. The World Trade Organization (WTO) and its predecessor, the General Agreement on Tariffs and Trades (GATT), supervise international trade agreements and work toward fewer restrictions in trade. The WTO is not a part of the United Nations, but the two organizations work closely together in areas of common interest. The UN Conference on Trade and Development (UNTAD) parallels the WTO in that it too is trying to encourage international trade.

Several other global organizations associated with the United Nations are also involved with economic globalization. They include the International Monetary Fund (IMF) and the World Bank. These specialized agencies help arrange the flow of money between countries, setting up

The world's economy can no longer be separated by national boundaries.

Many large corporations do business all around the world.

Chapter One—What Is Globalization?

loans, for example, from richer countries to poorer ones. They deal with *exchange rates*, and they work with *third-world countries* to end poverty and improve standards of living.

Political Globalization

The idea of political globalization has to do with an increasing number of international organizations that oversee global policies. Although countries make their own laws and decisions, they are held to certain international standards. For example, almost all the countries in the world are members of the United Nations and have signed the Charter of the United Nations. This means they are responsible for following the principles set out in that charter. They have also accepted the United Nations' Universal Declaration of Human Rights. Although this declaration is not legally binding, it points to common goals for the nations of the world. When countries do commit terrible human rights violations, these acts can be addressed by the United Nations.

Some see political globalization happening as democracy is put forward by the United Nations as the best political system. The goal of the United Nations is that all people have a voice in the directions their nations take. UN Secretary-General Kofi Annan has said, "When the United Nations can truly call itself a community of democracies, the Charter's noble ideals of protecting human rights and promoting 'social progress in larger freedoms' will have been brought much closer." Giving people a voice in the governing of their own country—democracy—satisfies one of the basic human rights laid out by the Charter of the United Nations and the Universal Declaration of Human Rights.

Globalization and Labor

Globalization can be seen in the area of labor and employment, as well. Labor globalization is connected with economic globalization in many ways. One tie is multinational corporations—huge businesses with offices all over the world. These corporations are involved with economic and trade concerns, but also affect labor globalization. Usually based in developed countries, such as the United States, these multinational corporations both sell goods and services around the world and hire employees at their branch offices and factories.

Since labor is generally cheaper in less developed countries, many multinational corporations prefer to operate most of their business in these countries. Corporations can increase their profits by hiring workers for less money. This practice is sometimes called outsourcing. Workers in developed countries usually dislike outsourcing, since the practice means fewer, or lower paying, jobs for local employees.

When forged money crosses borders, it becomes an international crime.

Chapter One—What Is Globalization?

Globalization and Crime

Globalization has many positive effects—but sometimes it has negative ones as well. Crime is always an issue at the local level, but it can also be a global problem. Quicker means of transportation allow for goods—often illegal drugs—to be carried from country to country. Often drugs are manufactured in countries with fewer regulations and then smuggled into wealthier, industrialized nations.

Smuggling is the main type of global crime, since it involves illegally bringing goods or people across international borders. People-smuggling usually concerns bringing illegal immigrants into a country—those who could not or were not willing to go through the regular legal channels to enter that country. Less often, the practice involves sneaking wanted criminals out of the country in which they have an outstanding arrest warrant. Sometimes people-smuggling includes the additional crime of *forgery* and false identification papers.

The Internet has led to another kind of global crime. Since information from the Internet is available worldwide, people sometimes use it to commit crimes across national borders. Such crimes include frauds and scams of various kinds (for example, trying to raise money for charities that do not exist), identity theft, and the distribution of child pornography. Since not all countries have the same laws, and because of the anonymous nature of the Internet, these criminals can be very difficult to capture and prosecute. Movie, music, and software *piracy* has also become a large problem globally. This happens, for example, when a movie is illegally copied and sold.

These are only a few types of globalization. With technology such as the Internet leading to more information on international topics, and with easier transportation, the world is becoming increasingly globalized. Nowadays, the Earth seems like a much smaller place than it did centuries ago. More areas of international life now intersect than ever before. While this is simply a description of the world we live in, globalization can have far-reaching effects—both good and bad. For example, the world's environment is greatly affected by globalization.

Pollution knows no boundaries.

Chapter 2

Globalization and the Environment

More and more people are becoming concerned about the environment, but it's a problem that has been around for thousands of years. People, looking for land where they could plant crops, cleared large amounts of forests. With the trees gone, the soil eroded more easily, blowing away during droughts, falling into the ocean along coastlines, and being carried away by rivers. As people gathered into large cities, air and water pollution became noticeable. Wood smoke and then coal smoke made the air thick and hard to breathe. Garbage and human waste littered the streets and contaminated rivers.

As the Earth becomes more crowded, erosion becomes a more serious problem.

Chapter Two—Globalization and the Environment

> The stated purpose of UNEP is "to provide leadership and encourage partnership in caring for the environment by inspiring, informing, and enabling nations and peoples to improve their quality of life without compromising that of future generations."

Clouds of polluted smoke from industrial smokestacks blow across international borders. So do billowing sandstorms. Rivers flow from country to country, carrying with them sediments and toxins. No country on earth can claim that its environmental policies and actions affect only its own citizens.

The world's population has reached nearly six and a half billion. So many people simply living and using the Earth's resources cannot help but have an effect on the environment. Industrialized nations tend to use more resources and add more pollution to the air and water, but poorer countries contribute as well (for example, through burning large amounts of trees to clear land for farming).

In the past, people took what they needed from the Earth, and often did not worry about **conservation**. The world seemed huge, and many thought they would never run out of land or clean drinking water. If the soil in one place became eroded or stopped growing crops as well, the people could always move somewhere else. There were always some people—or even entire societies—who tried to live in harmony with the Earth, but the issue did not become urgent until recent times. As the world's population increased, and as technological advances demanded more and more from the Earth, more people realized they must learn to care for the Earth if it was going to be around to provide for future generations.

United Nations Environment Programme

When the United Nations was founded in 1945, no specific mention was made of environmental issues, but in the 1960s and '70s, a new environmental awareness grew among people. The idea that caring for the environment was a global concern grew as well. The Charter of the United Nations stated that the organization wanted "to promote social progress and better standards of life in larger freedom"—and eventually, the United Nations realized that "better standards of life" needed to include protection of the Earth, since environmental conditions played such a large part in shaping people's lives.

The UN and Cultural Globalization: One World, Many People

From the "Stockholm Declaration"

"A point has been reached in history when we must shape our actions throughout the world with a more prudent care for their environmental consequences. Through ignorance or indifference we can do massive and irreversible harm to the earthly environment on which our life and well-being depend. Conversely, through fuller knowledge and wiser action, we can achieve for ourselves and our posterity a better life in an environment more in keeping with human needs and hopes. There are broad vistas for the enhancement of environmental quality and the creation of a good life. What is needed is an enthusiastic but calm state of mind and intense but orderly work. For the purpose of attaining freedom in the world of nature, man must use knowledge to build, in collaboration with nature, a better environment. To defend and improve the human environment for present and future generations has become an imperative goal for mankind—a goal to be pursued together with, and in harmony with, the established and fundamental goals of peace and of worldwide economic and social development."

In 1972, the United Nations held the UN Conference on the Human Environment in Stockholm, Sweden. This was the first major international meeting at which global environmental issues were discussed and the role of the international community was recognized. As a result of the Stockholm Conference, the United Nations founded the United Nations Environmental Programme (UNEP).

A major document created at the Stockholm Conference was the Declaration on the United Nations Conference on the Human Environment, often called the Stockholm Declaration. The Stockholm Declaration lists seven proclamations and twenty-six principles that guide the actions of the United Nations in environmental issues. These principles cover issues such as economic and social development, as well as strictly environmental concerns. For example, Principle 10 states:

> For the developing countries, stability of prices and adequate earnings for primary commodities and raw materials are essential to environmental management, since economic factors as well as ecological processes must be taken into account.

Since its creation in 1972, UNEP has grown into a major part of the United Nations. The organization monitors sixteen different environmental issues, ranging from freshwater to climate

Human well-being cannot be separated from the Earth's well-being.

The world's forests need protection.

Chapter Two—Globalization and the Environment

change to sports and environment. Eight divisions also operate within UNEP, dealing with things like environmental policy and public information.

Rio Earth Summit

In 1992, the United Nations Conference on Environment and Development (UNCED)—better known as the Earth Summit—was held in Rio de Janeiro, Brazil. Held twenty years after the Stockholm Convention, the Earth Summit was a massive conference, with representatives from 172 countries attending, over a hundred of them heads of state. For the first time, the majority of the world's governments acknowledged the need for real change in environmental policy in order to protect the Earth for future generations.

Five major documents came out of the Rio Earth Summit:

- the Rio Declaration on Environment and Development
- Agenda 21
- the Convention on Biological Diversity
- the Statement of Forest Principles
- the Framework Convention on Climate Change

The Rio Declaration built on the Stockholm Declaration, listing twenty-seven principles "working towards international agreements which respect the interests of all and protect the integrity of the global environmental and developmental system."

Whereas the Rio Declaration listed general principles such as "Human beings are at the centre of concerns for sustainable development. They are entitled to a healthy and productive life in harmony with nature," Agenda 21 was more detailed. Agenda 21 listed specific issues, like "Combating Poverty" and "Protection of the Atmosphere," then listed a series of goals for each issue together with actions to be taken by governments to improve problem areas.

The issue of ***deforestation*** was of particular concern at the Earth Summit. This interest led to the Statement of Forest Principles, a document devoted entirely to the supervision and protection of the world's forests. "Efforts should be undertaken towards the ***greening*** of the world," the document stated. "All countries, notably developed countries, should take positive and transparent action towards ***reforestation***, ***afforestation*** and forest conservation, as appropriate."

The Rio Declaration, Agenda 21, and the Statement of Forest Principles were not legally binding on the international community. Two other documents were produced at the Earth Summit,

Greenhouse gas emissions may bring about global warming.

Chapter Two—Globalization and the Environment

though, that were legally binding. These international treaties (called conventions) were the United Nations Convention on Biological Diversity and the United Nations Framework Convention on Climate Change. Biological Diversity, often called biodiversity, refers to the variety of different plants and animals living on the Earth. The purpose of the Convention on Biological Diversity was to protect the Earth's biodiversity.

The main goal of the Framework Convention on Climate Change was to reduce **greenhouse gas emissions** many scientists fear could lead to global warming. The original convention did not set the emission limits, but allowed for later additions, called protocols. In 1997, a meeting in Japan produced the Kyoto Protocol, which set the limits on greenhouse gas production. The Kyoto Protocol required that, between 2008 and 2012, countries reduce their 1990 levels of emissions by 5.2 percent. The Kyoto Protocol is very **controversial**, especially among industry owners, since these reductions would require major expenses and changes in their businesses.

United Nations Division for Sustainable Development

At the Rio Earth Summit in 1992, the United Nations founded the Commission on Sustainable Development. The job of the commission is to monitor the progress of the actions set out in Agenda 21 and to think of ideas to better carry out those actions.

The commission is led by the United Nations Division for Sustainable Development (UNDSD), itself a part of the UN Economic and Social Development Council. The mission of the UNDSD is "development that meets the needs of the present without compromising the ability of future generations to meet their own needs." The UNDSD works closely with UNEP, since their interests overlap to such a great extent.

The UN's concern with global issues naturally developed into a major interest in caring for the Earth and its natural resources. The United Nations strongly believes that we must look after the Earth's resources so they will be around for people to enjoy in the future.

The UN's interest in the environment comes out of its primary interest in human beings. This primary interest shows itself in the organization's contribution to taking care of the health needs of the world's people.

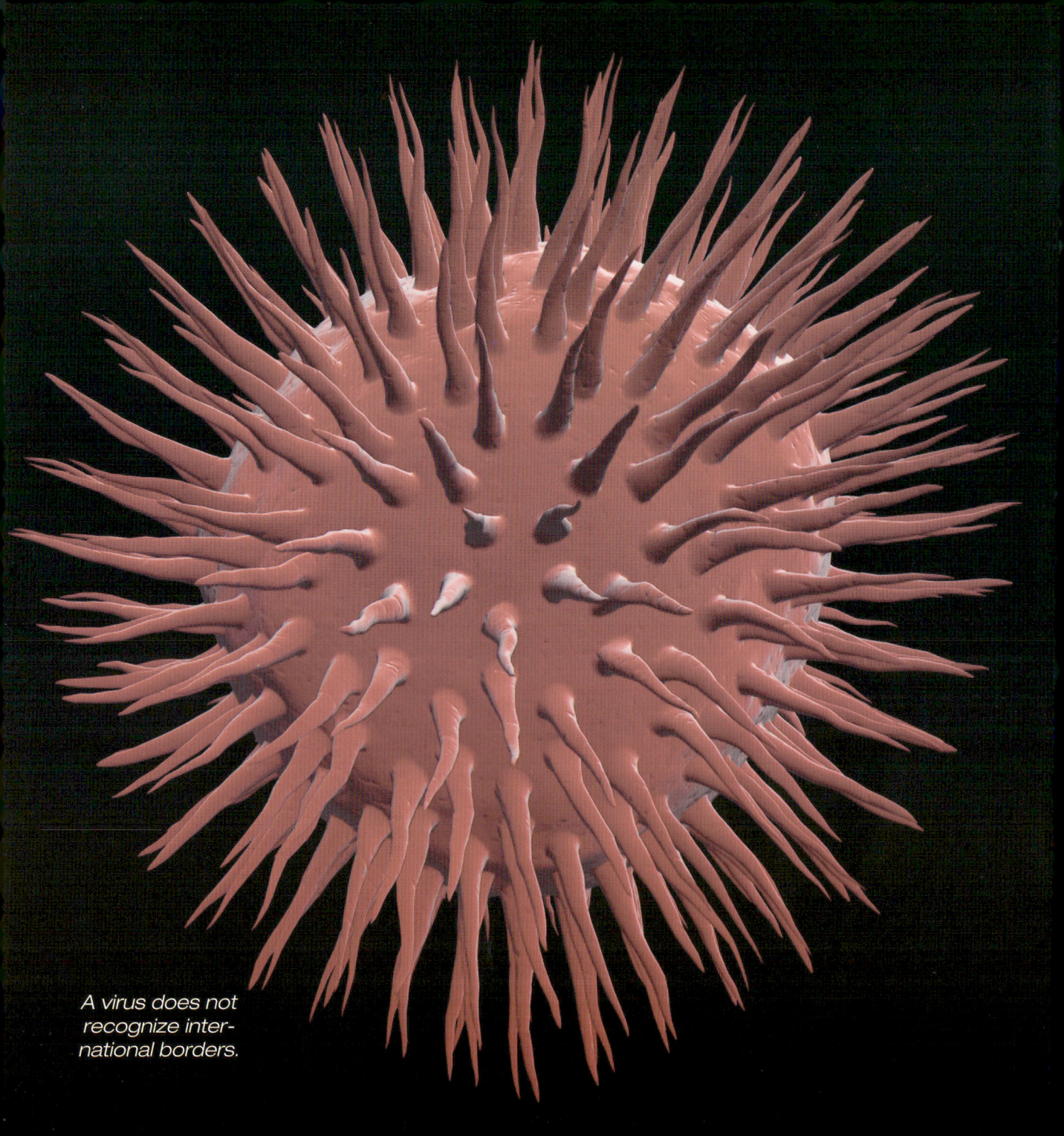

A virus does not recognize international borders.

Chapter 3

Globalization and Health

Diseases have never recognized international borders. They can be carried through air and water, passed on from person to person, or spread by the bites of infected animals. The United Nations is concerned with all areas of global health issues. These issues include both stopping the spread of infectious diseases and making sure that people have better access in general to health care and the tools they need to live healthy lives.

A medieval illustration of the Black Death, which killed nearly one-third of Europe's population.

Chapter Three—Globalization and Health

The Epidemic on the Roads

Although most might not think of it as a health problem, WHO has become very concerned with reducing the number of traffic accidents and the injuries due to those accidents. Many injuries from these accidents could be easily avoided by using seatbelts or proper child safety seats. A serious problem is also accidents between vehicles and pedestrians. Pedestrians are usually unprotected from such collisions. In 2004, WHO dedicated World Health Day (April 7) to road safety. In a resolution put out the same year, the organization recommended countries take specific steps toward decreasing the number of injuries and deaths related to traffic accidents. These steps would include better education about the risks of using alcohol, drugs, or cell phones while driving and stricter regulations on the use of safety equipment and the enforcing of these restrictions.

Global Epidemics

History tells the stories of dozens of plagues and outbreaks of disease. For centuries, these epidemics were restrained by the limits of travel. Sometimes, a disease was so deadly it killed people too quickly to spread very far; people who caught the disease died before they could travel and spread it.

More often, the type of travel available at the time limited the epidemic. For example, the Black Death spread across Europe in the fourteenth century, killing nearly a third of the population. Merchants and other travelers moving on foot, on horseback, or by boat carried the disease around the continent. In the twentieth century, soldiers returning home after the First World War spread a deadly form of influenza around the world. Since travel was so much quicker and easier in the 1900s than it was in the 1300s, the disease was able to affect millions more people than it would have centuries earlier.

Bacteria and viruses are not the only cause of global epidemics, though. Many argue that the influence of Western culture has created an epidemic of obesity and heart disease. People in industrialized nations tend to eat diets high in fats and sugars, which bring about a whole set of health problems.

In developing nations, on the other hand, the health epidemics are more often due to poverty and lack of adequate medical care. For example, in Africa and Asia, HIV/AIDS has struck millions

The UN and Cultural Globalization: One World, Many People

of people. Health-care workers struggle to help educate people on how to prevent the disease, as well as to treat those already infected. Another problem faced by very poor countries is the deaths of women in childbirth. In 2005, the chances of women dying in childbirth in parts of Africa were one thousand times greater than in developed countries.

The World Health Organization

The World Health Organization (WHO) is a part of the United Nations and focuses on health concerns of all kinds. Its stated goal is "the *attainment* of all peoples of the highest possible level of health." Many medical officers and scientists work for WHO, overseeing hundreds of different health issues, from *smallpox* to depression. These health issues also include positive steps toward better health, such as nutrition and diagnostic techniques and procedures—for example, X-rays and *ultrasounds*.

WHO workers oversee hundreds of different health issues.

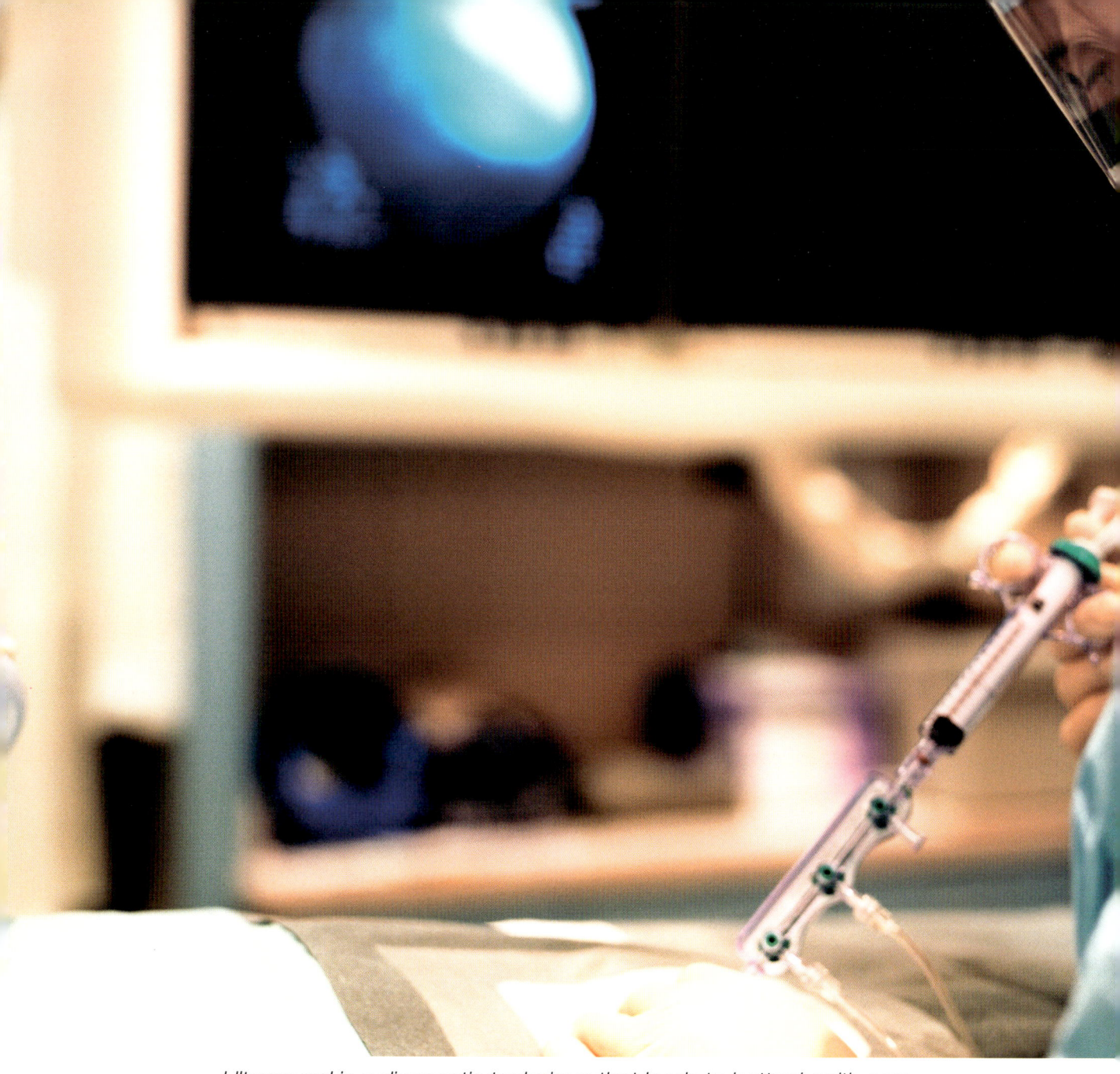

Ultrasound is a diagnostic technique that leads to better health care.

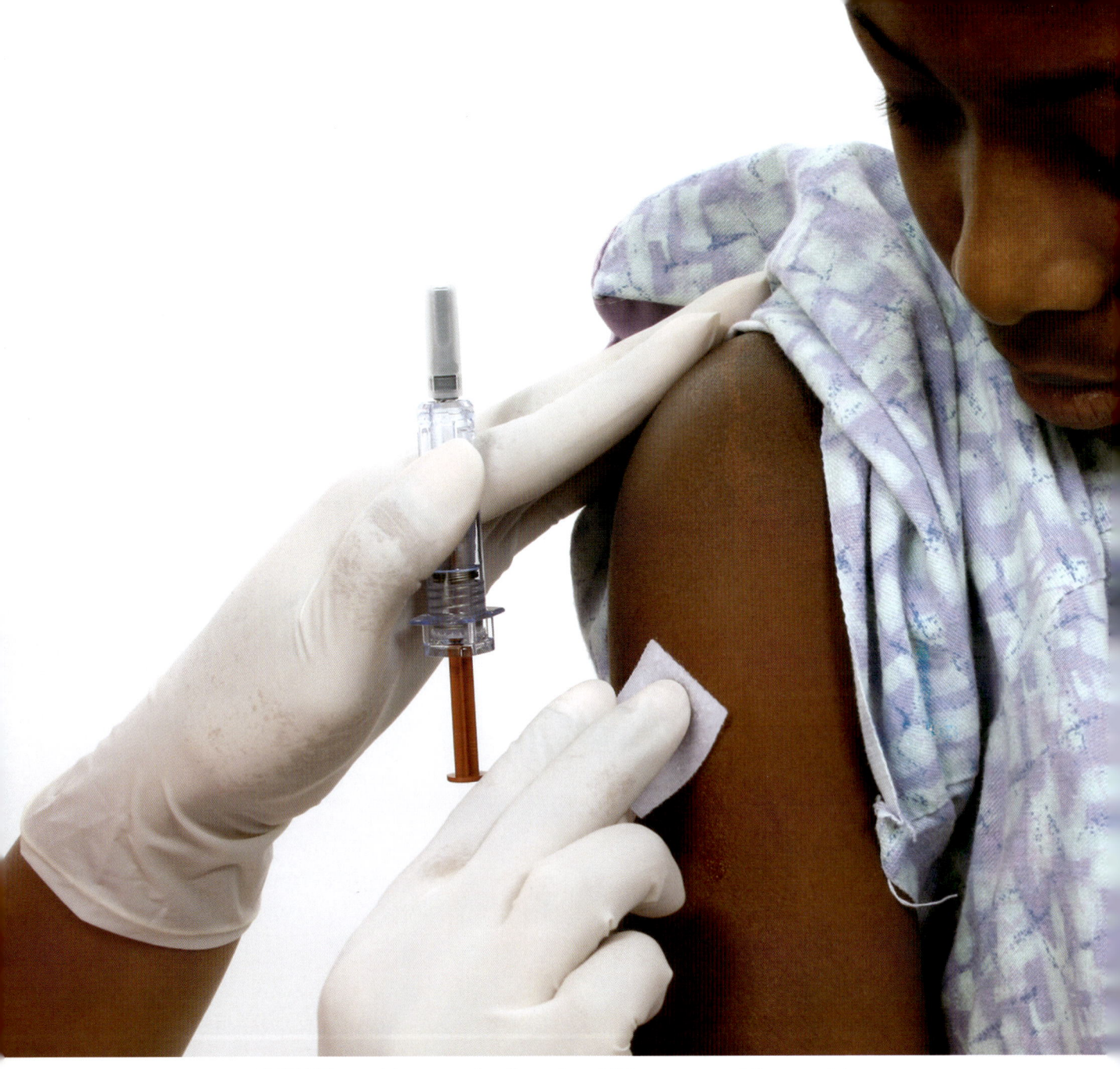

UNICEF provides vaccinations to children around the world.

Chapter Three—Globalization and Health

Due to the overlapping nature of UN agencies, the work of WHO often intersects with the work of other agencies. For example, at least a dozen UN agencies, including WHO, are involved in helping the Asian people after the tsunami of December 2004. Many agencies also come together to assist during famines. In these two situations, the agencies work closely with the United Nations Office for the Coordination of Humanitarian Affairs (OCHA). The agencies deal with different aspects of the disaster or emergency situation, with WHO taking care of the health concerns, and, for example, the United Nations Children's Fund (UNICEF) focusing on the children involved in the crisis, while the United Nations World Food Programme (WFP) brings in supplies to feed the hungry.

For WHO, globalization is a mixed blessing. As the world becomes more connected, the nature of disease threats changes. Diseases spread extremely quickly among industrialized nations, because of the frequent travel between countries. This makes serious outbreaks more difficult to control and isolate and means that doctors must work more quickly to stop the spread of the disease. On the other hand, globalization has increased the flow of medical supplies across borders. WHO has the organizational structure to be able to quickly send teams of medical personnel to sites of disease outbreak or health crises like famines or natural disasters.

As WHO takes on scores of health issues across the globe, it continually comes face to face with one overwhelming problem. Poverty is not only a problem in itself, but contributes to many of the world's health issues.

Poverty is a worldwide problem.

Chapter 4

Globalization and Poverty

In the world today, three billion people—nearly half the population of the Earth—live on the equivalent of less than two dollars a day. Over a billion have nowhere to get clean drinking water. Extreme poverty, when people cannot afford to buy even basic necessities such as food, is found throughout the world, sometimes among large numbers of people in the poorest countries but also in the richest countries as well.

People who live in poverty have less access to educational opportunities.

Chapter Four—Globalization and Poverty

International Day for the Eradication of Poverty

Beginning in 1993, the General Assembly of the United Nations decided to hold an annual International Day for the Eradication of Poverty. Every year on October 17, the nations of the world pay tribute to those living in extreme poverty. This yearly emphasis serves as a reminder of the large goal the United Nations and the people of the world want to achieve—the goal of completely ridding the world of poverty.

The ceremonies on this day usually include stories, essays, and songs by young people, as well as speeches and a panel discussion on some aspect of poverty. The goal of the International Day for the Eradication of Poverty is a greater awareness of the misery poverty causes, how it steals from people their basic freedoms and human rights, and how it must not be tolerated.

Poverty is an issue that affects and is affected by many other issues. For instance, poor people are less likely to get adequate health care and therefore often suffer from diseases and conditions not usually seen in developed countries. Trade is another difficult issue in very poor countries. These countries find it hard to be competitive in the international market. Frequently, they do not have the resources to sell that would help boost their country's economy. Cheaper, foreign-made goods take business from local merchants and industries, hurting the economy.

People living in poverty usually have limited access to education. Sometimes they are not able to go to school at all, while other times their schooling is inadequate. Nearly a billion people were illiterate as of 2000. Without education, and especially without being able to read or write, a person is generally not able to rise out of poverty and improve life circumstances.

The number of people living in extreme poverty over the last century has not changed as much as the gap between the incomes of the rich and the poor people of the world. According to the 1999 Human Development Report of the UNDP, in 1997, the richest 20 percent of people in the world earned seventy-four times as much as the poorest 20 percent. This inequality has risen sharply; in 1960, the richest 20 percent earned only thirty times as much as the poorest 20 percent.

The United Nations Development Programme

Although most United Nations agencies deal with poverty in some way, the UNDP is the most directly concerned with the issue. UNDP's Web site states that it is "an organization advocating

The UN and Cultural Globalization: One World, Many People

for change and connecting countries to knowledge, experience and resources to help people build a better life." Helping people build better lives is also a very central part of the Charter of the United Nations and the Universal Declaration of Human Rights. UNDP works to make this a reality by dealing with five general areas, one of which is poverty reduction.

In August of 2002, UNDP created the International Poverty Center in Brasilia, Brazil. The purpose of the International Poverty Center is to focus completely on poverty reduction. The center gathers information on poverty throughout the world, teaches officials how to use the information, publishes papers on poverty, and holds lectures and discussions on poverty-related topics. The center is not responsible for actually making or enforcing policies that would lead to poverty reduction, but instead it has the task of making sure those who do make policies have all the information they need to make informed decisions.

United Nations Decade for the Eradication of Poverty

The United Nations is very concerned with ending poverty and helping people live better, more fulfilling lives. Secretary-General Kofi Annan said that "whenever we lift one soul from a life of poverty, we are defending human rights. And whenever we fail in this mission, we are failing human rights." The mission of the United Nations is to promote "peace and security, development and human rights around the world"; ending poverty would be a gigantic step toward fulfilling all these goals.

In December 1995, the General Assembly of the United Nations named the years between 1997 and 2006 as the United Nations Decade for the Eradication of Poverty. The theme of the decade was "eradicating poverty is an ethical, social, political and economic imperative of humankind." To accomplish this mission, the United Nations promised to work with those living in poverty to help improve their way of life, not to simply give them handouts of food or other goods. One expert, reporting to the United Nations Commission on Human Rights, said:

> It is essential to set in motion machinery for participation which involves the poorest at every stage of the policies devised to help them. Only thus can concrete and lasting results be achieved. Only as they rediscover their full range of rights and freedoms shall we see emerging in all their splendor the human beings behind the poverty-scarred faces.

Fighting poverty is also fighting for human rights.

Poverty cannot end without the support of the entire world.

Chapter Four—Globalization and Poverty

Progress Toward Ending Poverty

Since poverty is such a complex issue, with many causes and affected by many issues, bringing all people out of poverty and helping them live better lives is a very difficult job. One step toward ending poverty is giving everyone the chance to go to school, at least at the primary level, so they can learn to read and write, can learn simple math skills, and can learn something about the world. These skills give people a huge boost toward being able to make something better out of their own lives. Education is not always enough to overcome poverty, of course, but without basic educational skills, leaving poverty behind becomes almost impossible.

In 2000, all the UN Member States committed to eight Millennium Development Goals. These goals were to be met by 2015. Many of them related to poverty, either directly or indirectly; for example, the first goal is: "Eradicate extreme poverty and hunger." The subpoints under this first goal are:

- "reduce by half the proportion of people living on less than one U.S. dollar a day"
- "reduce by half the proportion of people who suffer from hunger"
- "increase the amount of food for those who suffer from hunger"

Since the United Nations committed to these goals, much of its focus has gone into meeting them by the target date. UN committees exist whose entire purpose is to monitor the progress of the Millennium Development Goals.

At the 2004 International Day for the Eradication of Poverty, UN Secretary-General Kofi Annan reported on the steps that had been made toward ending poverty. He divided developing countries into three groups, those who have made good progress and are on their way to meeting all the Millennium Development Goals, those who have made progress on some but not all the goals, and those who have not made progress on most of the goals. North Africa and most of Asia fall into the first group; West Asia, Latin America, and the Caribbean fall into the second group; and the countries of sub-Saharan Africa—one of the poorest areas in the world—fall into the third group. Annan urged countries in the developed world to put a greater emphasis on their strategies for helping poorer nations, since without the complete cooperation of the wealthiest nations of the world, these Millennium Development Goals cannot be met. Poverty is a global problem, and it will take the support of the entire world to end it.

Poverty is such a gigantic problem that it is easy to get lost in statistics and numbers, sometimes forgetting that behind those staggeringly huge numbers are real people, each with a name and a

Poverty steals the most basic human rights.

Chapter Four—Globalization and Poverty

unique story they could tell about their lives. Kofi Annan wrote:

> Intent as we are on drawing up a solid statistical picture of our gains and shortfalls, let us also remember that our concern is not numbers but individuals: young people at work and out of school, children orphaned by AIDS and other preventable diseases, mothers who die in childbirth, communities affected by environmental degradation. It is well within our power to overcome these and other terrible manifestations of poverty and underdevelopment.

Poverty destroys people's basic human rights and freedoms, taking away their ability to choose the directions their lives will take. Freedom to choose one's religion is one right people have struggled with for thousands of years, in industrialized nations as well as in developing ones.

Globalization brings many religions to many nations.

Chapter 5

Globalization and Religion

The world is filled with many religions. Many of these religions have welcomed the process of globalization, taking advantage of a more connected world to spread the news of their beliefs to other people. On the other hand, as the world has become increasingly globalized, some religious groups have started to worry that the spread of cultural ideas and values might be harmful to their beliefs. They worry about cultural differences being swept away and wonder if soon all diversity will be gone. They speculate that the people of the world will all start to act and think in the same ways. They fear that the distinctiveness of their own religion might be lost.

The UN and Cultural Globalization: One World, Many People

These fears sometimes lead people to become very **nationalistic**, promoting their own culture and nation over global concerns. While there is nothing wrong with patriotism to a certain extent, some **extremists** react violently and launch attacks against other countries and peoples. Addressing this issue, UN Secretary-General Kofi Annan said:

> Religious practices and beliefs are among the phenomena that define us as human. . . . [But] religion has often been yoked to nationalism, stoking the flames of violent conflict. . . . Religious leaders have not always spoken out when their voices could have helped combat hatred and persecution.

The Millennium World Peace Summit of Religious and Spiritual Leaders

In August of 2000, two thousand religious leaders from all over the world came together at the United Nations headquarters in New York City to discuss how the religions of the world could make an impact on world peace. Although the Summit was not an official UN-sponsored conference, it was associated with the United Nations, and the Secretary-General spoke at the gathering. The Summit was organized largely by Bawa Jain, an **advocate** of interfaith dialogues, and funded by billionaire Ted Turner and his United Nations Foundation, an organization dedicated to assisting the work of the United Nations. The organizers of the Summit hoped that by bringing together representatives from over fifteen major faiths, world religious leaders could begin to talk about ways to end religious fighting and help bring peace to the world.

At the opening of the convention, Bawa Jain, Secretary General of the Summit, listed a number of goals he hoped the gathering would accomplish. He asked all delegates to sign a Commitment to Global Peace, and he proposed creating a council of religious leaders to work with the United Nations. From the United Nations, Jain asked for three things: for another World Peace Summit of Religious and Spiritual Leaders to be held every ten years, the creation of an Office of Religious Affairs at the United Nations, and partnership with a Council of Religious and Spiritual Leaders.

The delegates who attended the Summit were frustrated that the meetings mainly consisted of discussing general ideas instead of specific plans of action. Some felt no real progress was made toward solving actual problems. Despite this, the Summit produced several clear results. The Web

Religious beliefs are a part of what makes us human.

The UN and Cultural Globalization: One World, Many People

The Permanent Forum on Indigenous Issues

Indigenous peoples are native peoples with unique cultures, living as minorities in the midst of other cultures. They include Native American populations but also groups of native peoples throughout the world. In 2000, the United Nations created a Permanent Forum on Indigenous Issues to advise the Economic and Social Council of the United Nations on native peoples' issues and how best to address them. Part of this task includes preserving indigenous cultures, including native religions. Indigenous religions were also included in the Millennium World Peace Summit of Religious and Spiritual Leaders.

site of the World Council of Religious Leaders—itself formed as a product of the Millennium World Peace Summit—lists seven outcomes of the Summit:

- the signing of the Commitment to Global Peace
- initiation of a process to form a World Council of Religious and Spiritual Leaders
- cofounding of the Religious Leaders Initiative of the World Economic Forum
- a partnership with the United Nations' High Commission for Human Rights
- establishment of a Global Commission for the Preservation of Sacred Sites
- the opening of international interfaith dialogue
- the Congress on the Preservation of Religious Diversity

The Commitment to Global Peace condemned "all violence perpetrated in the name of religion" and acknowledged "the value of religious and ethnic diversity." Hundreds of the delegates signed the nonbinding statement at the Summit, and afterward the document continued to circulate throughout the world, collecting the signatures of religious and spiritual leaders. Among its objectives, the Commitment to Global Peace included, "To lead humanity by word and deed in a renewed commitment to ethical and spiritual values, which include a deep sense of respect for all life and for each person's inherent dignity and right to live in a world free of violence."

One aspect of the Millennium World Peace Summit not accepted by all delegates or religious groups was the statement by several leaders, including Bawa Jain, that all religions are equal. Jain stated that he believes people of all religions get their insights from the same source and that the outward appearance of religions is not important. Although some delegates approved of this idea,

Religious faith should increase the respect for all life.

Religion should build openness and peace, rather than prejudice and violence.

Chapter Five—Globalization and Religion

others, including the delegation representing the Roman Catholic Church, objected. While most agreed that religious leaders should work together to help the cause of world peace, many denied that to do so they must declare all religions equal.

The United Nations and Religion

Traditionally, the United Nations has avoided the topic of religion. Toward the end of the twentieth century, though, the United Nations has become more associated with interfaith dialogues, hoping to use the power of religion and religious beliefs in people's lives to help further the goals of the United Nations. To this end, the United Nations hosted the Millennium World Peace Summit of Religious and Spiritual Leaders, and UN Secretary-General Kofi Annan spoke at the Summit.

One way the United Nations has always been concerned with religion, however, is in the area of human rights. The Universal Declaration of Human Rights, adopted in 1948, states:

> Everyone has the right to freedom of thought, conscience and religion; this right includes freedom to change his religion or belief, and freedom, either alone or in community with others and in public or private, to manifest his religion or belief in teaching, practice, worship and observance.

In 1946, the United Nations created the Commission on Human Rights. The commission's job was to oversee all areas of human rights. In 1986, the commission appointed a Special Rapporteur of the Commission on Human Rights on Freedom of Religion or Belief. The Special Rapporteur is an individual whose job is to monitor religious freedom and "to examine incidents and governmental actions in all parts of the world which were inconsistent with the provisions of the Declaration on the Elimination of All Forms of Intolerance and of Discrimination Based on Religion or Belief, and to recommend remedial measures for such situations." The Special Rapporteur then reports to the Commission on Human Rights and to the General Assembly of the United Nations.

The process of globalization has affected religion simply because religious groups now have greater contact with each other. This contact has brought about conflicts and wars in the past, as people encountered those with beliefs very different from their own convictions. More recently, many have begun to realize that religious leaders can choose to guide their followers into more

Freedom of religion is one of the most basic of human rights.

Chapter Five—Globalization and Religion

constructive encounters with those of different religions. Interfaith groups, often working closely with the United Nations, have brought together leaders from many religions to discuss how they can help the cause of world peace.

The United Nations is concerned that globalization not take away people's freedom of religion. The United Nations, dealing with globalization on many levels, often finds it must make a determined effort to maximize the positive aspects of globalization while minimizing the negative aspects.

Many nations work together within the United Nations.

Chapter 6

Globalization and the United Nations

The United Nations is a massive global organization, with many divisions and suborganizations dealing with dozens of world issues. Since the United Nations is so involved with international affairs, much of what the organization does affects cultural globalization. The job of the United Nations is to work with the countries of the world to bring about peaceful resolution to conflicts and to help people live better lives. As countries communicate with each other more and work together with greater understanding, the process of globalization unavoidably speeds up.

The UN and Cultural Globalization: One World, Many People

One effect of such globalization has been the need for increased international regulations. Although all countries have different laws, frequent international connections have led to the development of international law governing these interactions.

International Law

In general, international law can mean one of two things: laws dealing with nations and the conflicts between them, or the laws affecting the legal disputes between two private citizens from different countries. The second of these two is usually called private international law, which does not always have set laws governing legal interactions. Generally, the people involved in the lawsuit must choose which country's courts will hear the case. The Hague Conference on Private International Law has worked for over a century to **standardize** laws affecting private citizens.

The Hague Conference is not an organization of the United Nations, but often works closely with the United Nations to create guiding legal policies. Some major Hague agreements (called conventions) have included declarations on international child abductions and determining which country's laws take precedence in situations such as product **liability** and traffic accidents between people of different nationalities.

As a global organization, the United Nations is much more involved with the laws dealing with relationships between countries than with those dealing with individuals. In 1947, the United Nations formed the International Law Commission to look into legal questions and put together recommendations about what is needed to be made into law.

International Court of Justice

One of the principle bodies of the United Nations is the International Court of Justice (ICJ)—often called the World Court—based in The Hague in the Netherlands. The ICJ has two main tasks: to resolve legal disputes between nations and to give opinions on legal questions asked by international agencies. The results of the first are legally binding, while the opinions given are not legally binding. Many international treaties include clauses stating that the ICJ will decide any disagreements that occur due to the treaty. However, the ICJ has no power to make sure its verdicts are carried out and must, like most courts, rely on other organizations to uphold its rulings. The General Assembly or the Security Council of the United Nations has the power to take actions against countries if it chooses, for example, by imposing economic sanctions against them.

The International Court of Justice is in the Peace Palace in The Hague.

The UN and Cultural Globalization: One World, Many People

> ## Cases Under Investigation by the International Criminal Court
>
> In 2005, three situations were under investigation by the ICC:
>
> 1. The Darfur region of the Sudan
> The Sudanese government and army were accused of widespread crimes against the people of the Darfur region. The International Commission of Inquiry on Darfur reported in January of 2005 that "government forces and militias conducted indiscriminate attacks" and that "the extensive destruction and displacement have resulted in a loss of livelihood and means of survival for countless women, men and children."
> 2. Northern Uganda
> The leaders of the Lord's Resistance Army (a rebel group fighting against the Ugandan government) committed crimes.
> 3. Democratic Republic of the Congo
> Conflicts within the DRC have led to thousands of atrocities and murders.

One of the weaknesses of the ICJ, though, is that at times, one party will refuse to abide by the verdict. If, for example, the refusing party is one of the five permanent members of the Security Council—and therefore can *veto* any decision—nothing can be done. This was the case in 1984 when the ICJ ruled that the United States had used unlawful force against the government of Nicaragua. The court ordered the United States to pay *reparations* to Nicaragua, but America refused.

Since its creation in 1946, the ICJ has made rulings on ninety cases and given twenty-five advisory opinions. As of 2005, the court had eleven open cases. These cases include border disputes, questions of *sovereignty*, and accusations of *genocide*.

International Criminal Court

In 2002, the United Nations established the International Criminal Court (ICC) to try people accused of genocide, war crimes, and crimes against humanity. The ICJ took care of judging the

Chapter Six—Globalization and the United Nations

Principles of the Global Compact

human rights
- the support and respect of the protection of international human rights
- the refusal to participate or condone human rights abuses

labor
- the support of freedom of association and the recognition of the right to collective bargaining
- the abolition of compulsory labor
- the abolition of child labor
- the elimination of discrimination in employment and occupation

environment
- the implementation of a precautionary and effective program for environmental *issues*
- initiatives that demonstrate environmental responsibility
- the promotion of the diffusion of environmentally friendly technologies

anticorruption
- the promotion and adoption of initiatives to counter all forms of corruption, including extortion and bribery

responsibility of nations, but had no authority over the individuals accused of such serious crimes.

Although established by the United Nations through the Rome Statute, the ICC now functions as an independent organization. The court works closely with the United Nations, but is not directly governed by it. Not all the 191 UN member nations have chosen to **ratify** the ICC statute. As of 2005, ninety-nine countries had ratified the statute, while another forty-one had signed but not ratified it. Countries refusing to accept the ICC include the United States, China, and Israel. The United States claims it will not be held accountable to the ICC because it fears other countries that dislike the United States will bring "frivolous or politically motivated prosecutions" against it.

Either a country or the UN Security Council must refer the cases on which the court rules. As of the middle of 2005, the ICC had received three referrals of situations from countries and one from the UN Security Council. The prosecutor of the ICC had opened investigations into three of these situations.

The United Nations works to make the Earth better for all human beings.

Chapter Six—Globalization and the United Nations

The Global Compact

While international organizations such as the ICJ and the ICC deal with globalization in terms of legal and criminal questions, the Global Compact addresses issues in the business world. The Global Compact—sometimes called the World Pact—began in 2000 as an opportunity for large corporations to come together and discuss globalization issues. Corporations that become members promise to make changes in their business practices to better align with the ten principles of the Global Compact. As of 2004, nearly two thousand companies from around the world had joined.

The principles of the Global Compact are similar to the goals laid out in the Charter of the United Nations. They include the support of human rights and anticorruption, as well as guidelines in the areas of labor and environmental practices.

Some human rights groups have been wary of the Global Compact, stating that the principles of the United Nations do not line up with the aims of large corporations. They fear the greed and the drive toward money-making often found in businesses could corrupt the United Nations and that some dishonest companies could use their membership in the Global Compact as a shield to protect their corrupt business practices. The United Nations, on the other hand, believes corporations can work in partnership with them to achieve the same goals and make the Earth a better place for all people.

As a global organization, the United Nations is very concerned with all aspects of globalization. With nearly all nations of the world as members, the United Nations can work with most of the world to create solutions for global problems. Organizations such as the ICJ, the ICC, and the Global Compact help the United Nations to end human rights violations and find ways to deal with other global issues.

Although the United Nations has many ideals, many of these principles have not been realized. In the near future, the United Nations has plans to strengthen the organization and make reforms to address problems within its own walls.

The United Nations works together to find solutions to the world's problems.

Chapter 7

The Future of the United Nations

Since its creation, the United Nations has had critics. While most people agree that the goals set out by the United Nations, such as world peace, are good, they disagree on whether the United Nations is doing an effective job of reaching them. The size of the United Nations sometimes makes it difficult for the organization to act, since there are thousands of people working in hundreds of different committees. Many argue that most of what the United Nations does is talk about issues, rather than actually solve problems. While this is a valid complaint in some areas, other branches of the United Nations are actively working toward global solutions.

The UN and Cultural Globalization: One World, Many People

United Nations Reform

When Kofi Annan became Secretary-General of the United Nations in 1997, he quickly presented the General Assembly with a package of reforms for the United Nations. Since then, Annan has proposed other changes to modernize the United Nations. Some of these have been carried out, such as consolidating three departments to create the Department of Economic and Social Affairs. Annan believes the United Nations must be constantly reevaluated and updated in order to function in the best way possible.

In 2005, Annan released a report called "In Larger Freedom: Toward Development, Security and Human Rights for All." In this report, Annan wrote:

> As the world's only universal body with a mandate to address security, development and human rights issues, the United Nations bears a special burden. As globalization shrinks distances around the globe and these issues become increasingly interconnected, the comparative advantages of the United Nations become ever more evident. So too, however, do some of its real weaknesses. From overhauling basic management practices and building a more transparent, efficient and effective United Nations system to revamping our major intergovernmental institutions so that they reflect today's world and advance the priorities set forth in the present report, we must reshape the Organization in ways not previously imagined and with a boldness and speed not previously shown.

The United Nations Millennium Development Goals

"We will have time to reach the Millennium Development Goals—worldwide and in most, or even all, individual countries—but only if we break with business as usual. We cannot win overnight. Success will require sustained action across the entire decade between now and the deadline. It takes time to train the teachers, nurses and engineers; to build the roads, schools and hospitals; to grow the small and large businesses able to create the jobs and income needed. So we must start now. And we must more than double global development assistance over the next few years. Nothing less will help to achieve the Goals."
-Kofi Annan

Secretary-General Kofi Annan

The UN and Cultural Globalization: One World, Many People

In September of 2000, the members of the United Nations signed the Millennium Declaration, committing them to meeting eight Millennium Development Goals by 2015.

1. Eradicate extreme poverty and hunger.
   - Reduce by half the proportion of people living on less than a dollar a day.
   - Reduce by half the proportion of people who suffer from hunger.
2. Achieve universal primary education.
   - Ensure that all boys and girls complete a full course of primary schooling.
3. Promote gender equality and empower women.
   - Eliminate gender disparity in primary and secondary education preferably by 2005, and at all levels by 2015.
4. Reduce child mortality.
   - Reduce by two-thirds the mortality rate among children under five.
5. Improve maternal health.
   - Reduce by three-quarters the maternal mortality ratio.
6. Combat HIV/AIDS, malaria and other diseases.
   - Halt and begin to reverse the spread of HIV/AIDS.
   - Halt and begin to reverse the incidence of malaria and other major diseases.
7. Ensure environmental sustainability.
   - Integrate the principles of sustainable development into country policies and programs; reverse the loss of environmental resources.
   - Reduce by half the proportion of people without sustainable access to safe drinking water.
   - Achieve significant improvement in lives of at least 100 million slum dwellers, by 2020.
8. Develop a global partnership for development.
   - Develop further an open trading and financial system that is rule-based, predictable, and nondiscriminatory, includes a commitment to good governance, development and poverty reduction-nationally and internationally.
   - Address the least-developed countries' special needs. This includes tariff- and quota-free access for their exports; enhanced debt relief for heavily indebted poor countries; cancellation of official bilateral debt; and more generous official development assistance for countries committed to poverty reduction.
   - Address the special needs of landlocked and small-island developing nations.
   - Deal comprehensively with developing countries' debt problems through national and international measures to make debt sustainable in the long term.
   - In cooperation with the developing countries, develop decent and productive work for youth.

Chapter Seven—The Future of the United Nations

- In cooperation with pharmaceutical companies, provide access to affordable essential drugs in developing countries.
- In cooperation with the private sector, make available the benefits of new technologies—especially information and communications technologies.

"In Larger Freedom" is a five-year progress report on the Millennium Declaration of 2000, in which nations promised to meet certain specific Millennium Development Goals by 2015. In his statement to the General Assembly accompanying the release of the report, Annan said, "What is needed now is not more declarations or promises, but action to fulfill the promises already made."

The difficulty lies in getting 191 member countries of the United Nations to agree on actions to be taken and to work together to carry out these actions. Even though all these countries have signed the Charter of the United Nations and agree on the broad principles, they often have very different ideas about how these principles should be put into practice.

In 1994, Mozambicans waited to vote in a UN-assisted election.

The UN and Cultural Globalization: One World, Many People

Commitments from the Copenhagen Declaration

1. Create an economic, political, social, cultural and legal environment that will enable people to achieve social development.
2. Eradicate absolute poverty by a target date to be set by each country.
3. Support full employment as a basic policy goal.
4. Promote social integration based on the enhancement and protection of all human rights.
5. Achieve equality and equity between women and men.
6. Attain universal and equitable access to education and primary health care.
7. Accelerate the development of Africa and the least developed countries.
8. Ensure that structural adjustment programs include social development goals.
9. Increase resources allocated to social development.
10. Strengthen cooperation for social development through the UN.

A Stronger United Nations

The size and scope of the United Nations means that it can be awkward and unwieldy when trying to act quickly and decisively. Committees study an issue and then report to other committees, who write reports and make presentations to still higher-level committees. Strengthening the United Nations means, in part, streamlining the processes required to act, so that things can be accomplished more quickly and easily.

Another way Kofi Annan has proposed for making the United Nations stronger is to update the membership of the Security Council to better reflect the modern world. Security Council reforms would probably include an increase in the number of permanent Council members to include countries such as Germany, Japan, or Brazil, as well as African countries. None of the new permanent members would have the veto power of the original members.

Included in the reforms to strengthen the United Nations is a major renovation of the Commission on Human Rights. Although the commission began with the right goals, it has, in fact, become a place where atrocities and human rights violations are too often overlooked or even caused. Kofi Annan, in his report, "In Larger Freedom," wrote:

> Yet the Commission's capacity to perform its tasks has been increasingly undermined by its declining credibility and professionalism. In particular, States have sought membership of the Commission not to strengthen human rights but to protect themselves against criticism

The United Nations works to improve the lives of ordinary people around the world—like this grandfather and grandson in Rio de Janeiro, Brazil.

Eritrean women celebrate a UN-supervised referendum.

Chapter Seven—The Future of the United Nations

or to criticize others. As a result, a credibility deficit has developed, which casts a shadow on the reputation of the United Nations system as a whole.

Annan proposes replacing the Human Rights Commission with a Human Rights Council. The members of the Human Rights Council would be elected by the General Assembly.

The Copenhagen Declaration

In 1995, the United Nations Department of Economic and Social Affairs held a World Summit for Social Development in Copenhagen, Denmark. At the summit, delegates put together the Copenhagen Declaration on Social Development, containing ten commitments to address the issues of poverty, employment, and **social exclusion**. These commitments foreshadowed the broader Millennium Development Goals set out in 2000. They are similar to the Millennium Development Goals but contain some differences. While the United Nations pursues the Millennium Development Goals, the Department of Economic and Social Affairs continues to pursue the commitments listed in the Copenhagen Declaration. Every five years since the first meeting, world leaders have met to reevaluate the progress made toward the commitments.

In February 2005, delegates met to discuss the Copenhagen Declaration and determined that some steps had been taken toward meeting the commitments, although the improvements had been slower than they would have liked, especially in the poorest countries. The delegates reaffirmed their pledges to the commitments and to the Millennium Development Goals, stating:

> We reaffirm our will and commitment to continue implementing the Declaration and Programme of Action, in particular to eradicate poverty, promote full and productive employment and foster social integration to achieve stable, safe and just societies for all.

The world has become increasingly connected during the last century, and the United Nations, as a major global organization, must struggle to change and adapt to the world's changing needs. Secretary-General Kofi Annan has said that the United Nations is "a work in progress," constantly needing to be updated and improved. Often, the ideals of the United Nations have not been realized and good ideas have floundered in **bureaucratic** red tape. Despite its failures, the United Nations has continued to try and make the world a better place for all people, meeting the challenges of globalization and using the benefits these connections have brought. To fully meet its goals, the United Nations will need the support of all the world's countries and leaders.

Time Line

1946	UN Commission on Human Rights is established.
1946	International Court of Justice is created.
1947	International Law Commission is formed.
1948	Universal Declaration of Human Rights is adopted.
1972	UN Conference on the Human Environment takes place in Stockholm, Sweden.
1972	United Nations Environmental Programme (UNEP) is founded.
1979	WHO declares smallpox eradicated.
1986	Special Rapporteur of the Commission on Human Rights on Freedom of Religion or Belief is appointed.
1992	UN Conference on Environment and Development takes place in Rio de Janeiro, Brazil (usually called the Earth Summit).
1992	United Nations Division for Sustainable Development (UNDSD) is founded.
Oct. 17, 1993	First annual International Day for the Eradication of Poverty takes place.
1995	World Summit for Social Development takes place in Copenhagen, Denmark.
1997	Kofi Annan becomes Secretary-General of the United Nations.
1997	The Kyoto Protocol calls for reductions in greenhouse gas emissions by 5.2 percent of 1990 levels.
1997–2006	United Nations Decade for the Eradication of Poverty.
2000	Millennium World Peace Summit of Religious and Spiritual Leaders.

2000	The Millennium Declaration sets out eight Millennium Development Goals to be met by 2015.
2000	Permanent Forum on Indigenous Issues is created.
2000	The Global Compact is created.
2002	International Poverty Center in Brasilia, Brazil, is created.
2002	International Criminal Court is established.
2006	The United Nations continues to work to improve the world for all people.

Glossary

advocate: Someone who acts and speaks on behalf of an issue.

afforestation: The conversion of land not previously forested into forest by planting trees.

attainment: Achievement of a goal.

bureaucratic: Having to do with the way administrative systems are organized.

conservation: The preservation, management, and care of natural and cultural resources.

controversial: Provoking strong disagreement or disapproval.

deforestation: The removal of trees from an area of land.

diplomatic: Concerned with international diplomacy—the practice of using negotiations rather than force to settle conflicts between nations—or the work of diplomats, those people who carry out such negotiations.

diversity: Variety.

exchange rates: The rates at which a unit of currency of one country can be exchanged for a unit of currency of another country.

extremists: Those who have extreme or radical political or religious beliefs.

forgery: The act of making or producing an illegal copy of something.

genocide: The systematic murder (or attempt to murder) an entire group of people.

greenhouse gas emissions: The expulsion into the air of gasses such as carbon dioxide and ozone that contribute to the warming of the Earth's atmosphere.

greening: Supporting the protection of the environment.

liability: Legal responsibility for something.

multiculturalism: The existence of the cultures of different countries, ethnic groups, or religions.

nationalistic: Relating to the extreme devotion to one nation and its interests above all others.

piracy: The taking and using of copyrighted or patented material without permission or legal right to do so.

ratify: To formally approve.

reforestation: To replant an area with trees after its original trees have been cut down.

reparations: Compensations demanded of a defeated nation by the victor in a war or conflict.

smallpox: A highly contagious disease caused by a virus and marked by high fever and formation of scar-producing pustules.

social exclusion: The state of being excluded from mainstream society and its advantages.

sovereignty: Self-rule.

standardize: To remove variations and irregularities and make all types or examples of something the same or bring them into conformity with each other.

third-world countries: Nations outside the capitalist industrial nations of the first world and the industrialized communist nations of the second world.

ultrasounds: Images produced by a technique that uses high-frequency sound waves reflecting off internal body parts.

veto: Reject.

Further Reading

Bowden, Ron. *World Poverty*. Chicago: Raintree Library, 2003.

Connolly, Sean. *Safeguarding the Environment*. North Mankato, Minn.: Smart Apple Media, 2005.

Foley, Ronan. *World Health: The Impact on Our Lives*. Chicago: Raintree Library, 2003.

Hibbert, Adam. *Globalization*. Chicago: Raintree Library, 2005.

January, Brendan. *Globalize It!* Minneapolis, Minn.: Twenty-First Century Books, 2003.

Maddocks, Steven. *World Hunger*. Milwaukee, Wis.: Gareth Stevens Publishing, 2004.

McGowan, Keith. *Human Rights*. San Diego, Calif.: Lucent Books, 2002.

Osborne, Mary Pope. *One World, Many Religions: The Ways We Worship*. New York: Knopf Books for Young Readers, 1996.

Pollard, Michael. *United Nations*. New York: New Discovery Books, 2005.

Watson, Susan. *Living Sustainably*. North Mankato, Minn.: Smart Apple Media, 2003.

For More Information

Earth Summit
www.un.org/geninfo/bp/enviro.html

The Global Compact
www.un.org/Depts/ptd/global.htm

Global Issues
www.globalissues.org/

The Globalization Web site
www.sociology.emory.edu/globalization/

International Court of Justice
www.icj-cij.org/icjwww/icjhome.htm

International Criminal Court
www.icc-cpi.int/home.html&l=en

Millennium World Peace Summit
www.millenniumpeacesummit.com/mwps_about.html

One Planet, Many People
www.na.unep.net/OnePlanetManyPeople/index.php

Poverty: An Obstacle to Human Rights
www.un.org/rights/poverty/poverty5.htm

A World Connected
www.aworldconnected.org/

World Health Organization (WHO)
www.who.int/en/

Publisher's note:
The Web sites listed on theses pages were active at the time of publication. The publisher is not responsible for Web sites that have changed their addresses or discontinued operation since the date of publication. The publisher will review and update the Web-site list upon each reprint.

Reports and Projects

- Write about one major environmental problem facing some part of the world today. Tell how globalization has improved the problem or made it worse.
- Imagine you are a young person living in poverty in some area of the world. Research what life would be like for you and write a journal entry telling about it.
- Make a list of the major diseases the World Health Organization is working to eradicate.
- Do a presentation in front of the class showing how the world has become more globalized in the last hundred years.
- Tell your class about a world religion. Describe how globalization has affected this religion.

Bibliography

"10 Commitments." *Earth Summit 2002.* http://www.earthsummit2002.org/wssd/10commitments/10commitments.htm.

Annan, Kofi. *In Larger Freedom: Towards Security, Development and Human Rights for All.* September 2005. http://www.un.org/largerfreedom/index.html.

"A Brief Introduction to the UN Convention on Biological Diversity." *IISB Linkages.* February 10, 2002. http://www.iisd.ca/biodiv/cbdintro.html.

Carnegie Council on Ethics and International Affairs. "Additional Resources: 'Environmental Rights.'" *Human Rights Dialogue: Environmental Rights.* 2005. http://www.carnegiecouncil.org/viewMedia.php/prmTemplateID/8/prmID/4976.

CorpWatch. http://www.corpwatch.org.

Environmental History Timeline. http://www.radford.edu/~wkovarik/envhist/.

Federal Office for Spatial Development, Switzerland. "1972: UN Conference on the Human Environment, Stockholm." *Sustainable Development.* December 7, 2004. http://www.are.admin.ch/are/en/nachhaltig/international_uno/unterseite02329.

Institute for Humane Studies, George Mason University. *A World Connected.* http://www.aworldconnected.org.

International Court of Justice. http://www.icj-cij.org/icjwww/icjhome.htm.

International Criminal Court. 2005. http://www.icc-cpi.int/home.html&l=en.

Keefer, Evergreen. *Jihad vs McWorld: Whose Paradise is Lost in Civilisation's War on Terror?* 2002. http://www.nyu.edu/classes/keefer/hell/hell01.html.

Kelman, Naamah. "Globalization and Religion." *World Council of Churches.* 1999. http://www.wcc-coe.org/wcc/what/interreligious/cd33-12.html.

Lechner, Frank. *The Globalization Website.* 2000. http://www.sociology.emory.edu/globalization.

Novaes, Eduardo Sales. "Agenda 21: Background." *Brazil: Environment.* http://www.mre.gov.br/cdbrasil/itamaraty/web/ingles/meioamb/agenda21/anteced/index.htm.

Office of the United Nations High Commissioner for Human Rights. "Human Rights Dimension of Poverty." *Issues: Poverty.* 2004. http://www.ohchr.org/english/issues/poverty.

Office of the United Nations High Commission for Human Rights. Issues: *Special Rapporteur of the Commission on Human Rights on Freedom of Religion or Belief.* 2004. http://www.ohchr.org/english/issues/religion.

Schoenfeld, Stuart. "The Environmentalists' Narrative." *The Sustainability Report.* 2004. http://www.sustreport.org/resource/shoenfeld.html.

"The Secretary General Statement to the General Assembly." March 21, 2005. http://www.un.org/largerfreedom/sg-statement.html.

Shah, Anup. "Causes of Poverty: Poverty Facts and Stats." *Global Issues.* June 11, 2005. http://www.globalissues.org/TradeRelated/Facts.asp#1.

Trafford, Paul. *Glimpses of the Presentations at the Millennium World Peace Summit of Religious and Spiritual Leaders.* October 1, 2000. http://www.chezpaul.org.uk/interfth/summit/speeches.htm.

United Nations Department of Public Information. "UN Conference on Environment and Development (1992)." *Earth Summit.* May 23, 1997. http://www.un.org/geninfo/bp/enviro.html.

United Nations Department of Public Information. *Environmental Resources in the United Nations System.* 2005. http://www.un.org/issues/m-envir.asp.

United Nations Department of Public Information. *International Day for the Eradication of Poverty.* Oct. 1998. http://www.un.org/rights/poverty/poverty5.htm.

United Nations Division for Sustainable Development. 2005. http://www.un.org/esa/sustdev.

United Nations Environment Programme. http://www.unep.org/.

United Nations Environment Programme. *One Planet, Many People: Atlas of Our Changing Environment.* 2005. http://www.na.unep.net/OnePlanetManyPeople/index.php.

United Nations General Assembly. *Report of the United Nations Conference on Environment and Development.* 14 Aug. 1992. http://www.un.org/documents/ga/conf151/aconf15126-3annex3.htm.

United Nations Procurement Service. *Global Compact.* 2005. http://www.un.org/Depts/ptd/global.htm.

UN Millennium Development Goals. 2005. http://www.un.org/esa/sustdev.

The World Council of Religious Leaders. 2000. http://www.millenniumpeacesummit.com/mwps_about.html.

World Health Organization. 2005. http://www.who.int/en.

"World Summit for Social Development: Introduction." *Economic and Social Development at the United Nations.* 21 Aug. 2000. http://www.un.org/esa/socdev/wssd/agreements/poachi.htm.

Index

afforestation 25
Africa 11, 31, 32, 70
Annan, Kofi 15, 48, 66–67, 70, 73
Asia 31, 35

Black Death 30–31
Brazil 25, 40, 71

Canada 12
child pornography 17

deforestation 25
Denmark 73

epidemic 31
extremists 48

famine 35
forgery 17

genocide 60
global warming 26
greenhouse gas emissions 26–27

Hague, The 58-59
HIV/AIDS 31, 45, 68

identity theft 17
indigenous 50
influenza 31
International Monetary Fund (IMF) 12
Internet 10–11, 17

Japan 27

Mexico 12
Middle East 11

natural disasters 35
Nicaragua 60

outsourcing 15

piracy 17
plague 31
pollution 18-21
poverty 36–46, 70, 73

reforestation 25

smallpox 32
sovereignty 60
Sweden 22

tsunami 35

United Nations
    Agenda 21 25
    Charter 15, 40, 69
    Children's Fund (UNICEF) 35
    Commission on Human Rights 40, 53
    Commitment to Global Peace 48, 50
    Conference on Environment and
        Development (UNCED) 25
    Conference on the Human Environment 22
    Conference on Trade and Development
        (UNTAD) 12
    Congress on the Preservation of Religious
        Diversity 50
    Convention on Biological Diversity 25, 27

United Nations (*cont.*)
- Coordination of Humanitarian Affairs (OCHA) 35
- Copenhagen Declaration on Social Development 73
- Council of Religious and Spiritual Leaders 48
- Department of Economic and Social Affairs 73
- Development Programme (UNDP) 39–40
- Earth Summit 25
- Economic and Social Development Council (UNDSD) 27, 66
- Environment Programme (UNEP) 21–22, 27
- Framework Convention on Climate Change 25, 27
- General Agreement on Tariffs and Trades (GATT) 12
- General Assembly 39, 40, 53, 66
- Global Commission for the Preservation of Sacred Sites 50
- Global Compact 63
- High Commission for Human Rights 50
- International Court of Justice (ICJ) 58–60, 63
- International Criminal Court (ICC) 60–61, 63
- Kyoto Protocol 27
- Millenium Development Goals 43, 68–69, 73
- Millenium World Peace Summit 48, 50
- Office of Religious Affairs 48
- Rio Declaration on Environment and Development 25
- Secretary-General 15, 48, 66, 67, 73
- Security Council 60, 61, 70
- Statement of Forest Principles 25
- Stockholm Declaration 22, 25
- Universal Declaration of Human Rights 15
- World Court 58
- World Food Programme (WFP) 35
- World Health Organization (WHO) 31–32, 35
- World Peace Summit of Religious and Spiritual Leaders 48, 53
- World Summit for Social Development 73

United States 11, 60–61

veto 60

World Bank 12
World Trade Organization (WTO) 12
World War I 31

Picture Credits

Corel: pp. 69, 71, 72
iStock
    Alan Heartfield: p. 24
    Jaimie Duplass: p. 34
    Konstantinos Kokkinis: p. 64
    Lisa Kyle Young: p. 59
    Michael Osterrieder: p. 28
    Patrick Roherty: p. 36
    Simon Moran: p. 16
    Stephen Everett: p. 13
    Wael Hamdan: p. 46
Jupiter Images: pp. 8, 10, 14, 18, 20, 23, 26, 33, 34, 49, 51, 52, 54, 56, 62
PhotoSpin: pp. 38, 41, 42, 44
United Nations: p. 67

To the best knowledge of the publisher, all other images are in the public domain. If any image has been inadvertently uncredited, please notify Harding House Publishing Service, Vestal, New York 13850, so that rectification can be made for future printings.

Biographies

Author

Sheila Nelson has written a number of educational books for young people. She lives in Rochester, New York, with her husband and children.

Series Consultant

Bruce Russett is Dean Acheson Professor of Political Science at Yale University and editor of the *Journal of Conflict Resolution*. He has taught or researched at Columbia, Harvard, M.I.T., Michigan, and North Carolina in the United States, and educational institutions in Belgium, Britain, Israel, Japan, and the Netherlands. He has been president of the International Studies Association and the Peace Science Society, holds an honorary doctorate from Uppsala University in Sweden. He was principal adviser to the U.S. Catholic Bishops for their pastoral letter on nuclear deterrence in 1985, and co-directed the staff for the 1995 Ford Foundation Report, *The United Nations in Its Second Half Century*. He has served as editor of the *Journal of Conflict Resolution* since 1973. The twenty-five books he has published include *The Once and Future Security Council* (1997), *Triangulating Peace: Democracy, Interdependence, and International Organizations* (2001), *World Politics: The Menu for Choice* (8th edition 2006), and *Purpose and Policy in the Global Community* (2006).